A COLLECTION OF ESSAYS ON GLOBAL ISSUES IN REGARDS TO THE NATION OF SERBIA:

I0417422

Observing Serbian Domestic and Foreign Policy

PETER WILLIAMS, II

First Volume of the Series
Understanding Modern International Politics and Conflicts

Note to the Reader

"I do sincerely hope that the reader shall develop an interest from these writings in not only the country of Serbia, but the greater global battle for international security and freedom. It is in this battle that is not only fought with arms and weapons but with human thought. My prayer is that good shall prevail against the oppression brought against humanity."

-Peter J. Williams, II

"Peace is more than the absence of war. True peace is justice, true peace is freedom, and true peace dictates the recognition of human rights."

-Ronald Reagan

"Press forward. Do not stop, do not linger in your journey, but strive for the mark set before you."

-Pastor George Whitefield

Essay One: *Human Trafficking*

An Analysis on the Current Situation in the Balkans and the Serbian Government's relationship with the OSCE in regards to human trafficking

Since the end of the Cold War, Europe has seen an increase in human trafficking. The battle against human trafficking has grown tremendously. While an attitude of urgency to hasten the elimination of slavery is ever present among European authorities, and the OSCE has adopted initiatives to combat human trafficking, many member states have been slow to strengthen their institutions against transnational and internal human trafficking. Even as Governments address the issue in a variety of manners, organized trafficking networks respond by finding ways to circumvent the enforcement of the law. Several, if not most countries in Europe, suffer from a severe lack of prosecution and proper adjudication of human traffickers. Corruption in legal institutions has shown itself to be a number one threat to state's actions against human trafficking and solutions suggested by the OSCE, including the Action Plan to Combat

Trafficking in Human Beings (CTHB).

Serbia understands the situation very well. Herself and her neighbors are

victims of the horrific trade that has been using our region as a center for

human trafficking. According to gvnet.com—a website set up by the World

Bank —120,000 enslaved women and children pass through the Balkan

Peninsula every year. On those who are enslaved in the Serbian Province

of Vojvodina, an article from the BETA News Agency (August 7, 2006)

stated that "The victims are most commonly women from poor families

who were subjected to violence within their families. Their documents are

taken away and many times they are threatened to be killed or thrown

into the Danube River where no one will find them … The children, some

as young as three, are snatched from their parents and sold for as little as

£300."[1] Law Enforcement in the Balkans has also been subject to

corruption. In the Province of Kosovo in Southern Serbia, three UN Police

in the region were arrested (along with four foreigners) for participating

in Sex Trafficking.[2] For hundreds of families and communities in Slavic

communities in Eastern Europe, Human Trafficking has sadly become a

part of their life. As mentioned earlier, corruption in legal institutions has

continued to inhibit progress. In the past, the OSCE has formed several

---

[1] http://gvnet.com/humantrafficking/Serbia-Montenegro.htm
[2] http://web.archive.org/web/20070218221653/http:/www.isn.ethz.ch/news/sw/details.cfm?id=12681

initiatives to combat such corruption. Nethertheless, Serbia, along with her Balkan comrade Greece, have worked hard to combat such corruption and improve the legislative and prospective systems in regards to human trafficking. Many developing face challenges in this process, including Serbia. Greece passed her first law criminalizing human trafficking in 2002. Greek Law number 3064/2002 is important to the history of countering human trafficking via legislations because that law also ensured government support to reintegrate the victims, not just outlawing slavery and providing sentencing.[3] Serbia has taken legislative steps as well to address the issue.

The effectiveness of several initiatives addressing human trafficking has yet to either be implemented or successively addressed by the Serbian government. While Serbia has addressed human trafficking and begun programs to combat human trafficking, few are put into action. Regardless the Serbian government did take a step forward my funding educational programs. Serbia see the awareness and the education of human trafficking as an important solution and should be taken seriously by all member states. Serbia is delighted with the OSCE's effort to address the trustworthiness between NGO's and governments, as seen throughout the CTHB. Fostering trust between European and International organizations with European governments is another priority for the Serbian

---

[3] https://etd.ohiolink.edu/!etd.send_file?accession=osu1339617852&disposition=inline

authorities. Serbia has suffered from inadequate prosecution, and the Serbian Government and people seek for change to come in the near future. Serbia highly encourages that nations in the OSCE continue push for cooperation with NGO and UN organizations as well as allocate government funds towards educating the public, especially the youth, on human trafficking.

Essay Two: *Peacekeeping*

United Nations Peacekeeping efforts from the view of the Serbian Government

It is self evident that the United Nations, since its official establishment in 1945, has been a bastion of world peace and dedicated to ending conflicts globally. Over the years, UN peacekeepers have become a major force in the effort of international conflict resolving. Likewise, the basic ideology behind UN peacekeeping has been made clear throughout the history of the UN: Protecting human lives and resolving global tension/security threats at international levels. It is imperative that as a committee, these truths are understood by each member state, and furthermore, the world populations, especially those directly affected by UN operations. In past, UN peacekeeping missions have established two reputations: positive or negative. It is without doubt that past UN missions have provided aid to many groups of people and brought peaceful resolutions to many conflicts. However, multiple errors, mistakes, etc. made by UN peacekeepers have jeopardized the trustworthiness of the entire UN organization. Thus, our goal as a committee must be to define the role of peacekeeping in our changing society and bring reform to operations that will prevent catastrophes and better address conflicts. Nigeria is dedication to these goals, and to ensuring the protection of civilians from political or military corruption.

In order to understand peacekeeping, its development, and its place in the world, we must investigate the operations of peacekeepers since its earliest stages. The early missions of UN peacekeeping mainly involved maintaining ceasefires, providing beneficial support in political solutions to resolve conflicts. These operations were conducted in a style of peacekeeping limited to stabilizing the situations, primarily as observers; peacekeepers were generally lightly armed. UNTSO and UNMOGIP, the first peacekeeping operations, operate in this fashion. In 1956, UNEF, the first armed mission, was deployed to maintain the ceasefire in the Suez Canal Crisis. ONUC, UN operation in the Congo of 1960, ended with 250 deaths of UN personnel. This incident should, and is, considered a major catastrophe and a lesson for the UN. The UN learned that is not always beneficial for direct peacekeeping/military engagement. From this lesson, we must learn that a balance is necessary between each crisis between observation and armed enforcement of peace during war. After ONUC, the UN returned to establishing their missions under strict engagement regulations and to maintain ceasefire and UN buffer zones.[4] Then, after the end of the cold war, there was a surge of new missions developed across the world due to the end of rivalry in the security council. From this point, the UN shifted away from the traditional, previous form a

peacekeeping. We witnessed a dramatic change in the function of peacekeepers in conflict and underdeveloped zones. The growth in the number of missions aided many people and addressed many conflicts. However, at the same time many of these operations and tha however, at the same time many of these operations ended in failure, disaster, and even deaths, such as was seen in the Congo (ONUC). Furthermore, there was the case in Somalia when peacekeepers died from th furthermore, there was the case in some Malia when peacekeepers, from the United States, or killed while undergoing reconnaissance of the region.

---

[4] http://www.un.org/en/peacekeeping/operations/history.shtml

The UN, in the recent past, has begun to make steps towards addressing the problems with in peacekeeping operations as well as reforming the process. In October of 2014, the secretary general Ban Ki-Moon established an independent review board to assess the peacekeeping operations[5]. It is without doubt, after reviewing peacekeeping history, that the UN house done not enough to address necessary reform in peacekeeping operations. We have witnessed time and time again operations that were mandated by the Security Council prematurely and thus was not able to correctly carry out the peace process. Serbia is one of the largest contributors of peacekeeping troops in Europe. Furthermore the government and military of Serbia has, in the past decade, begun to work with United States within the Global peace operations initiative (GPOI), to expand regional and multinational peacekeeping[6]. Serbia strongly believes that with proper review, reform, and understanding of the foundation of peacekeeping, this committee can enable UN peacekeeping to address and solve the conflicts and tension in our society that hinder the well-being of all people.

---

[5] http://www.un.org/en/peacekeeping/operations/reform.shtml
[6] http://www.state.gov/t/pm/ppa/gpoi/.

Essay Three: *Cyberwarfare*

A Brief History with Cyberwarfare and the Serbian Government's Policy in regards to the topic

Our world is rapidly changing. Many aspects of our communities are developing and changing into very different conditions. The many societies of the world are becoming internationally linked together and the international community is becoming more and more connected than ever. Especially with cyber warfare and cyber-security in general, it is becoming increasingly evident that a universalistic society brings inherent benefits to the international populations as well as palpable and also hidden challenges, dangers, and security threats. Not only is the security of one organization or just one nation at risk, but, indeed, the entire world's [international] security is at risk. With all this mind, it is imperative for this committee to define the legal terms of cyberwarfare and cyber attack.

In 1988, the first recognised worm to affect the world's cyber infrastructures, the Morris worm, spread and attacked mainly U.S. computers. This would be only the beginning of hacker attacks on the global scale. *The American organization NASA experienced attacks and was even forced to block emails in 2006. That was done out of fear of further hackers gaining access to confidential material. Then only a year

later, Estonia was berated by a series of denial of service (DoS) attacks. The foreign cyber infringements of government networks began after previous controversy with Russia. It should noted that Estonia responded well with restarting some services within hours; "the attacks were more like cyber riots than crippling attacks" (*NATO review).

These attacks developed slowly in intensity and frequency, but in the past the international communities, especially the U.S. and Europe have experienced a rise in cyber security threats. Terrorist and non-state groups have been found responsible for more and more security breaches. Simultaneously, many governments are continuing grow in their participation in cyber attacks, as seen in 2007, when U.S. and China had their government networks breached almost entirely by state actors. Both state and non-state cyber attacks have harassed security of many governments. That State of Israel received a barrage of hackers against its internet infrastructure from non-state groups (Terrorist groups Hamas and Hezbollah suspected) in 2009. Time and time again, as the years progress, attacks are made and networks breached. The frequency of these attacks are becoming too hazardous to be ignored. The issues confronting this committing can be narrowed down to the following questions: how can we define cyber-security threats in war? How should this committee approach non-state versus state cyber attacks? How does

or should ideologies such as jus ad bellum and jus in bello influence our definitions and do the two address cyber warfare?

Little has been done by the UN to approach the issues or encourage/engage other nations to combat the threats posed by cyber attacks. This has to change. It is necessary for the UN to recognise the changing of society and advance with it to confront the issues raised with the rise of security threats. In 2011, December 9th, the UN organization

ECOSOC held an event specifically addressing cyberspace and cyber security. They recognised the vast changing world in relation to cyber threats and security. UNODA (United Nations Office of Disarmament Affairs) stated that UNIDIR convened a meeting entitled "Cyber Threats: Information as a Weapon?" It is time to go beyond discussion and create clear and definite approaches to cyber threats.

Serbia is a country molded by time, experience, and state-security restlessness. This delegate from Serbia understands security threats and recognises the need to combat cyber space's negative impact on the world. "In a country like Serbia, where more than 50% of the population has Internet access, citizens are increasingly relying on global IT networks in their daily life," said Peter Burkhard, Ambassador for the Organization for Security and Co-operation in Europe (OSCE). Europe and most of the world is much aware of the strife and tension in Serbia due to the

Serbian-Kosovo Conflict. Especially in the past months and years of fighting between us and the Kosovar rebels, cyber attacks have been increasingly. Hackers of been terrorising Serbian networks and infiltrating our systems. Despite efforts by our government, Serbia does not have a CERT (Computer Emergency Response Team). Chairman of the Information Association of Serbia, Nikola Markovic, stated at a cybersecurity conference in Belgrade, in 2015, that "Having CERT would help regional co-operation in the field of cyber security. Currently our regional partners do not know what to do with cyber-attack information they gather; how to share information or whom to alert in Serbia." (**2015, OSCE). This Delegate sees the need for immediate defining of cyber warfare and cyber attacks. Once again, Serbia is nation that understands war and cyberwar alike. The justification for war and self-defense of a state should strictly defined, ensuring peaceful results in all conflicts, as defined in Article 2 of the UN charter. Cyberware crimes should treated no differently than that of conventional war crimes already defined by the United Nations. As in all armed conflicts, certain measures are reached when securing national stability and security. Serbia understands these measures, as state well aware of war. An attack on a nation's security and well being is an act of war against peace and general stability of a state.

Essay four: *Wartime Internet Liberties*

Addressing rights of civilians to access the internet in regards to nations in

conflict

The freedom of speech in the internet should treated with urgency and a sense of high regard for its crucial influence and power over the international communities of people everywhere. Yes, indeed, with the internet, aspects such as humanitarian, censorship, war, etc. are within this debate. The discussion of specifically wartime access to the internet and of cyberspace is our debate and how it relates to the freedom of speech. We, this committee, have been bestowed with a great honor and responsibility. And that is to attempt to determine each sovereign state's' right to the internet, in times of conflict. It could be considered an unorthodox discussion for DISEC. Granted, with its benefits, we are to observe, understand, and determine the weapon of the internet. In times of war, it must be noted, the internet's position becomes increasingly and obviously influential. We are not debating tangible guns or the mobilization of arms. But yet, we are still observing a weapon. The weapon of the internet.Since the internet's creation, it has shown great promise to the international communities. It has shown the potential to liberate people across the globe with the gift of information, who previously would have known little about even the very place they live.

The internet is touching more and more people everyday. In Serbia, over

66% of our population has internet access as of 2015, which is a

significant jump with in the last decade, nearly doubling. The internet is a

powerful recourse, especially for the spreading of ideas and promoting

democracy. The International Human Rights Law (IHRL) was established

to protect all humans from injustice and create an international standard

for humanitarian ideology and legislation. Even so, Serbia testifies by the

state's own experience and by watching external events, the International

Law and even humanitarian laws of some countries have been openly

violated. The freedom of speech likewise has been limited unnecessarily

and for unlawful purposes by non-state groups and governments alike.

The UN has made advances in its policies to encourage and protect

humanitarian rights. However, the freedom of speech and the internet has

been only generally addressed and little has been done to achieve a

cohesive approach to the situation. Most humanitarian laws or standards

for protecting people's rights come from state legislation. As stated

previously, Serbia is and old country with a long history. The people of Serbia

know well the tragedies of both now and yesterday. Serbia is dedicated to the

proposition

and idea that God created men and women with divine calling and commission to be treated equally and with respect for one's divinely given rights. Serbia will forever

protect the humanitarian rights divinely grounded in the pillar of peace and of justice.In times of war, Serbia understands that the state must do what is lawfully necessary to protect the government and social well being. The internet, especially social media, can become a hinderance to a state's well being. Serbia believes that censorship in times of war is necessary and justified when done lawfully, and with certain limitations. However, there is a clear right of the freedom of the press and the freedom to assemble. Serbia does not wish to infringe with this right. The Serbian government is a leading nation in the balkans on promoting freedom of speech. On November 2, 2011, Prime Minister Mirko Cvetkovic stated that Serbia "fully respects, guarantees" the freedom of the press. The Serbian Government has worked hard to provide Serbs with their God given right of free-speech. Today, the Serbian government has no restrictions on the internet. For national protection, the internet (specifically emails) are monitored by the government. This committee must recognise the fine line and balance between protecting people from illicit media that promotes crime and general social instability and brutally murdering those who have the divine right to speak and assemble as free people. Our constitution reaffirms Serbian belief that the right of free speech

and press is a humanitarian right, while gives limitations for the government

restrictions when the protection of security or to "protect the rights of others"

and to "uphold authority." Serbia once again establishes that this delegate is

dedicated to the protection of humanitarian rights and the protection of national

security in times of war.

Previous Page: Collage of Photos of Serbian landscape, people, Belgrade,

and outline of Serbian borders with flag inside.

Essay four: *Serbia Overview*
An Essay exploring information for the reader.

Serbia as the state exists today is new, gaining its current form in 2006. Its history however is lengthy. Its homeland had been incorporated into three major empires of history, the Roman, Byzantine, and Ottoman Empires. Serbia also became the central conflict which sparked the Great War (World War I). The Serbs themselves have been on the seat of much controversial periods of European and Global history, The Serbs have been the crossroads of diverse people groups as well as religions, including Catholicism, Eastern Orthodox Christianity, and Islam. During the Ottoman reign over the territory, made young Serbian males were conscripted into elite Ottoman military guards. Undoubtedly, Serbia has been intertwined into the history of the Balkans and influenced many. With the rise of communism in Eastern Europe, and the increasing influence of the Soviet Union over her neighbors, Serbia too would be affected. At the time leading up to World War II, Serbia was not an independent state but a part of the Kingdom of Yugoslavia. This kingdom assembled a union

between the Croats, Serbs, and Slovenes, all of whom

had bitter rivalries, be based off ethnicity or religion. The Croats and

Slovenes, for instance were predominantly Roman Catholic and the Serbs

were Eastern Orthodox. Meanwhile, there remained a presence of muslims

in the country, This kind of complicated diversity was not new, and had

been in this manner for centuries. This union would survive after Hitler's

invasion, which forced the King (King Peter II) into exile, and develop into

a communist state. The map below shows the ethnic diversity during the

communist state of Yugoslavia. The communist state was then falling

apart, shortly following the official collapse of the USSR in 1992. Serbs had

become a majority of the Yugoslav state and Serbia began to assert its

power after the Bosnian government's declaration of independence from

Yugoslavia in 1992.The bitter war between the two groups culminated in

several massacres and brutal genocides of the Bosnians. To this day, the

scars remain and the tension is still reverberating between the two

groups.

The more recent major international event in Serbia was the independence of Kosovo, a self-proclaimed state that is considered by Serbia to be a part of their country, Again, the conflict was deeply

personal for the people engaged in the issue, involving both ethnicity and religion. The Kosovo War (1998-1999) was the beginning of the Kosovo armed fight for independence. The war saw NATO strikes on Serbia in order to pressure the government to release Kosovo.